D0090776

"It itches."

franklin habit

INTERWEAVE.
interweavebooks.com

For my parents, *who once said, "Mommy and Daddy are busy. Why don't you go draw for a little while?"*

and for my sister, *who once said, "Make me something."*

———

cover & interior design pamela norman

Text and illustrations © 2008 Franklin Habit
All rights reserved.

Interweave Press LLC
201 East Fourth Street
Loveland, CO 80537-5655 USA
interweavebooks.com

Printed in Canada by Friesens

Library of Congress Cataloging-in-Publication Data

Habit, Franklin, 1971-
It itches : a stash of knitting cartoons /
Franklin Habit, author. p. cm.
ISBN 978-1-59668-093-7 (hardcover)
1. Knitting--Caricatures and cartoons. 2. Knitting--Humor.
3. American wit and humor, Pictorial. I. Title.
NC1429.H23A4 2008
746.43'20207--dc22

2008026524

10 9 8 7 6 5 4 3 2

... and for your reading pleasure...

Work in Progress

during the process of preparing this neat little volume I have often been asked*:

Why? Why a book of knitting cartoons?

For the same reasons any guy would.

1. I'M TOO SHORT to make a living as a superstar ballerina.

2. MY PARENTS ARE nagging me for something to put in the annual family Christmas letter besides, "Franklin continues to elude capture by the CIA."

3. THERE WERE NO takers for a proposed book of taxidermy cartoons.

4. I'M BETTER AT drawing sheep than superheroes.

5. I WANTED TO recycle material from Give That Girl Some Needles, my short-lived off-Broadway musical about the life of Elizabeth Zimmermann.

6. YEARS SPENT LIVING among the herd have allowed me to observe and record the daily habits of skittish wild knitters with unparalleled freedom.

7. I NEED THE money to buy ~~food~~ yarn.

So here it is—my humble stash of knitting cartoons. I hope it makes you laugh. Because as Grandma said when I told her about it, "If this one does well, maybe next time they'll let you write a *real* book."

— *Franklin, Chicago, 2008*

* by Mom, who rather hoped I'd be a successful banker at this age.

It itches

"I incorporated your thoughts about last year's sweater into the design for this year's."

*"Well, here's your problem.
This isn't a lace chart, it's a Sudoku."*

*"What part of 'Do not open the stash cupboard'
was unclear to you, Edward?"*

Marge began to wonder whether she might have misread the pattern.

Lost Knitting Diaries of the Famous:
Selected Excerpts

Betsy Ross (1752–1836), *upholsterer and patriot*
Yesterdaye spent nine ful hours sewing ye flag of ye colonies when I would much prefer to be at my knittyng. Genl Washington stopt at noone to check my progress, at which hour I had saw fit to treat myself to a few rowes on ye new fleecy tippet. Ye good Genl seeing me thus not employd on ye flag for a fewe seckinds questiond my devotion to it, to which I replyd tartly that he could stick his blessd pointy starres into his eer. Wil begyn agayne on ye flag this morn after one more rowe.

Jane Austen (1775–1817), *novelist*
To-day spent several hours in selecting lambswool to become a new cap. The selection fair to middling. Much to the annoyance of the young man behind the counter there were agonies over which shade is most in harmony with both my complexion and my dress. Cassandra favored the rose, and I the white. In the end, could not choose one or the other. So purchased both, and some lovely fine cotton newly reduced.

Pledged with Cassandra as witness that I shall buy no more until my present supply is exhausted, though she seemed dubious of my sincerity. I have noticed that selecting knitting wools is much like selecting a husband; others are much more inclined to quickly narrow one's choices than one is oneself.

Edgar Allan Poe
(1809–1849), *writer*
The weather being very fine, I sat for some hours in the park to work the second of the pair of stockings I wish to give Lenore as a birthday gift. When for a moment my back was turned, its finished mate was plucked clean from my knitting basket by a large raven. I am sick at heart to think I shall see it nevermore. *(Note to self: poss. story idea here?)*

Thomas Alva Edison
(1847–1931), *inventor*
Stayed up far too late again knitting the second slipper. This morning my eyes ache from the strain of working under the gas jet. Cannot shake the thought of a world in which a brilliant, perpetual daylight would empower man to knit without ceasing.

Gertrude Stein (1874–1946),
writer and art connoisseur
Yesterday sitting and not knitting. Today sitting and knitting and knitting and knitting and sitting. Sitting and knitting round on the round, the round goes round and round and the round grows round and grows round while sitting and knitting. Hole then no hole then hole then no hole. Sitting and knitting holes and knitting no holes. Doily.

Friedrich Nietzsche
(1844–1900), *philosopher*
Discovered this afternoon a most terrible error early in the body of the splendid blue pullover at which I have been knitting. To fix it required ripping out the whole of the work, which took several hours, and beginning again. Oh, agony! Found this so invigorating that I plan to do the same with both sleeves.

Marcel Duchamp
(1887–1968), *artist*
Lunch today with Man Ray, with whom I shared my latest pattern for a scarf to be knit using a flagpole, a megaphone and a boa constrictor named Alphonse. He failed to grasp the irony. Cretin.

"In a minute. I'm almost at the end of the row."

"Of course I hate to say anything, but isn't Edna looking a little bulky since the baby?"

It itches

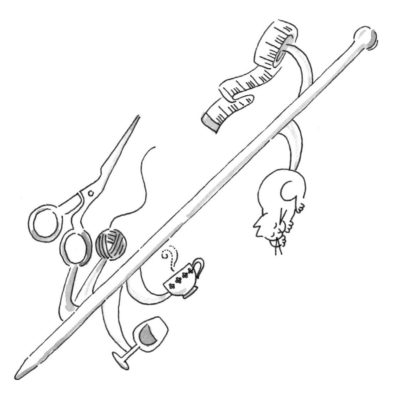

The Swiss Army Needle

"I told you this was a bad idea."

"These days I'm really into felting."

"So, we're all agreed. The knitting needles must go."

*"If it bothers you that much, Caitlin, then I suggest that you
and your teddy and your mid-Victorian ideas about gender
get the hell back to the other side of the playground."*

"I'll be the judge of that."

Monster in the Closet

I WAS POKING AROUND THE APARTMENT one morning, hunting for my lucky underwear, when I remembered it might have landed behind the sofa. Pushing the throw pillows to one side, I peered into the shadows and got the shock of my life.

Staring back at me was this . . . something. It was shapeless. Lumpy. Distinctly fuzzy. Mostly dark, but mottled with patches of bright color.

So I did what every red-blooded, urban male does when confronted by an unclassifiable, furry thing crouching be-hind the furniture. I screamed, and then I called the maintenance guy. Herbie showed up ten minutes later. I stood by nervously as he reached over the sofa and gingerly prodded the Whatsit with the end of a long screwdriver.

"What on earth *is* that?" I whispered.

"Beats me," said Herbie, giving another poke. There was a long, low growl.

"Can you can get rid of it?"

"I think you need a specialist," Herbie said, heading for the door.

Specialists didn't help. Animal control,

pest control, two biology professors, and a keeper from the city zoo all came and went, baffled. The thing, meanwhile, refused to budge and appeared to be growing steadily.

A month after the first sighting I showed up at knitting night with dark circles under my eyes and spilled the whole, sad tale. They laughed.

"This is not funny," I said. "If it gets any bigger, it might eat the coffee table."

"Not likely," said our Wise Old Knitter. "It sounds to me, young man, like what you have back there is a common or garden Stash."

"You know what it is?" I gasped. "Do you know how I can get rid of it?"

Wise Old Knitter glanced knowingly at the rest of the group. "My dear," she said, "you had better just learn to live with it."

She was correct, as usual. Years later, the Stash is still here, though it has migrated from the original nest near the sofa to more commodious digs in a large cupboard in the dining room. Though I am still wary, a thorough study of the available scientific literature has allowed us to achieve *entente cordiale*.

In case you should find yourself with a similar unbidden houseguest, here are a few useful facts I've gathered on the origins, habits, and life cycle of the species.

Reproduction. Researchers have been unable to ascertain whether the stash breeds through sexual activity or by simple division. However, it is fertile, adaptive, and widespread. Like *Rattus norvegicus*, the common brown rat, it has learned to thrive in every climate and nearly every land mass on earth. In certain parts of Canada, it is estimated that one is never further than ten feet from a full-grown stash.

Diet. The stash prefers to feed exclusively upon a diet of yarn, and will only take up residence in proximity to

although a well-fed specimen is generally benign, there are a few instances of fatal stash attack on record.

a ready supply. Fiber content makes no difference—it will munch as happily upon acrylic as upon cashmere.

Environment. The ideal stash breeding ground is a shady, secluded nook thickly covered with a mixture of partial skeins left over from finished projects; large, hasty purchases later regretted in the cool light of day; and odd balls acquired at prices that were just too ridiculously low to resist. Where such conditions exist, the arrival of a stash is almost inevitable.

Human Symbiosis. Because the stash is itself sedentary, it must be fed constantly by a human host in order to survive. It achieves this through hypnosis, compelling its accomplice to procure a steady supply of yarn while in a trance-like state. The human is often entirely unaware of the situation, until he checks his credit card statements at the end of the month and finds dozens or even hundreds of yarn shop charges he certainly didn't *intend* to make.

Extermination. Once established, the stash is nearly impossible to eradicate. There are several documented cases in which a knitter, determined to escape, has abandoned her home—only to find that the stash has followed.

And although a well-fed specimen is generally benign, there are a few instances of fatal stash attack on record. I found the following in the archives of the *Daily Bugle* of Pigeon Junction, Missouri:

Mrs. Bernadette Thorpe, 47, of Begonia Road, was apparently killed by a yarn stash that had been growing unchecked in her spare bedroom closet for 15 years. She was last seen by her husband, Wilberforce, heading upstairs with a large bag from a local yarn shop.

"I asked her why she had to go and buy more yarn," said Mr. Thorpe, "and she muttered something like, 'You don't understand, you will never understand.'

Then she closed the door and that was it."

Mr. Thorpe called the police after hearing a scream and a muffled thud from inside the locked bedroom. Upon investigation, officers discovered an 11-foot stash sprawled across the floor, but no sign of Bernadette Thorpe. The stash had apparently consumed her, along with a bag of 30% off discontinued powder blue alpaca worsted from Right Up Ewe Alley in St. Louis.

Mr. Thorpe says he is deeply saddened by the loss of his wife, <u>but he has taken up knitting to console himself.</u>

The emphasis, dear reader, is mine.

And I think I'll run along now and pick up a few fresh skeins—just to be on the safe side.

"Lisa, we need to talk."

Jackpot at the Lucky Knitter Casino.

"Is there anybody here who can teach me how to bind off?"

"Little Liza has her father's nose, but your colorway."

"I saw you across the pool and couldn't help
thinking of my dear old grandmother."

Crafty

ONE WINTER NIGHT OVER LOVELY warm drinks and even lovelier warmer wool, the conversation turned to the perennial puzzle of whether knitting is an art or a craft. I can't describe the resolution, unfortunately, because first somebody said "ergo" and then somebody else quoted Schopenhauer from memory and suddenly I was under the table in a fetal position with my fingers in my ears.

Not that my companions were dull or pompous. No. It's just that once, years ago, in an unguarded moment I let it slip that I think knitting could be fairly categorized as a craft. You can still see the scar where the sock needle punctured my neck.

I will sit with you from sunrise to last call and cheerfully debate knitting's *little* questions, such as the relative merits of flap versus short-row heels or whether it could ever be possible to own too much qiviut. But the weightier issues trigger flashbacks. Don't ask me to place your Fair Isle sweater on an imaginary gamut somewhere between decoupage and the *Mona Lisa*, unless you want to bring back the facial tic that medicine and meditation have finally gotten under control.

Here, and please put that sock needle down until I'm finished, is all I have to say on the subject.

According to my faithful dictionary, a craft is not a bad thing to be. Listen.

craft (n) *1. an occupation, trade, or activity requiring manual dexterity or artistic skill* (v) *1. to make or produce with care, skill, or ingenuity*

Sounds perfectly respectable, does it not? Even complimentary.

I grew up in a house full of crafts, crafting, and crafters. The crafter-in-chief was my mother, who tackled and mastered one medium after another: sewing, crochet, macramé, crewel, cross-stitch, quilting, cake decorating, upholstery.

Sometimes she may have gone a little too far. In the mid-1970s, we had five gigantic pieces of macramé in the living room alone, and to this day I'm paranoid about being spied on by those beady-eyed owls. But on the whole, she was an inspiration. Every time I pull out my knitting needles I draw on lessons learned while watching her at the craft table.

She taught me to be fearless and to ignore difficulty ratings. Who cares if the pattern book says the Sunbonnet Sue cake should only be attempted by persons holding a Black Belt in non-standard use of the star tube? You want the cake? You have two hands and at least half a brain? Make the cake. Or, as the case may be, the Aran pullover or the lace shawl.

She taught me to value the friendship of other creative people. Her best buddy, Shirley, has been her collaborator, supporter and enabler for twenty-five years. They've seen one another through kiln misfires, overcrowded charity bazaars, ungrateful children, and decades of holiday deadlines. They've taught, teased, inspired, and consoled each other. When I took my first, timid steps into the larger knitting community, that's what I hoped to find—and I did.

Best of all, she taught me that the joy of crafting is contagious. The only delight

dexterity and artistic skill were replaced by blunt scissors and bent pipe cleaners.

greater than wearing it or using it after you make it, is the joy of passing it along to others who will appreciate it.*

All good, no? And yet I have seen covens of otherwise peaceful knitters rise up as a seething, hissing tangle of fury when an outsider innocently refers to their beloved pastime using the "c" word. Why?

Because somewhere along the way the popular perception took a wrong turn. Dexterity and artistic skill were replaced by blunt scissors and bent pipe cleaners. Who, nowadays, does *craft projects*? Schoolchildren, nursing home residents, the inmates of psychiatric wards—people who are assumed to be less than fully capable, and who cannot choose to leave the room when ordered to make a

Thanksgiving centerpiece out of chicken feathers and a plastic cup.

So it stands to reason that if you call a knitter's gorgeously cabled sock a craft project, in her mind you're equating it with a tissue box cover made from Popsicle sticks. And you'd better duck and run.

Well, I'm not gonna take it anymore. "Craft" is too ancient, beautiful and noble a word to leave to the hacks at the less-inspired housekeeping magazines. My knitting is my craft; therefore, I am a craftsman. It's a badge I wear with pride. I made it myself.

---

* If they don't appreciate it, next time they get a gift certificate. Mom taught me that, too.

"It starts out kinda slow, but on row forty-six she throws in a plot twist that will just <u>kill</u> you."

"From beyond the grave, your grandmother's restless spirit cries out to know why that beautiful blue merino cardigan with the traveling cables is still in the back of your bottom drawer."

"You're cute, Rodney—but I never ply on the first date."

"Maybe you can fix that bit with blocking."

"I think I see where the clicking noise is coming from."

"And if Tommy will keep Mama's little secret, tomorrow
Mama will take Tommy to get some ice cream."

"On the other hand," thought Brenda, "I bet I could stash a couple of skeins in there."

Man vs Skein

GOOOOOOOOD MORNING, FIBER fans! It's a beautiful day here at the county fairgrounds and the gates have just opened on the tenth annual Sinking Meadows Sheep and Wool Festival. I'm Otis Hunnicutt, here in the booth with my good buddy Milton Culpepper—

Hey folks!

—and we'll be bringing you the play-by-play commentary on all the action in the market shed.

And boy howdy, Otis, doesn't it look like we're in for a thrilling day?

You said it, Milton. Only nine o'clock and already I've seen several near-collisions with those handpainted sock yarns from the Happy Bellwether.

I do believe you're right, Otis. In fact, it seems our first match is about to begin.

Who's this we're looking at, Milton?

Otis, that's Stan Petrie of Port Maxine. Stan's been a knitter for seventeen years and is a veteran of more than two dozen fiber festivals.

Wow! A real titan!

You betcha. What's more, last week he told the entire guild that he was only coming here to look around.

I've heard that one before.

Me too. I see Stan has entered the Krayzee for Ewe booth with his friend Betty, and he's squaring off against a skein of . . . what would you call that, Otis?

Milton, I'd call that a subtly variegated silk/wool blend in shades ranging from a watery eau de nil to a deep cobalt. And now he's petting it. Milton, Stan has just made first contact with the yarn.

Yes! It's on!

One, two, three—three strokes. And he's lifting it off the rack. This could spell trouble. Wait, no, he's putting it back and stepping away. But—

Interference! Betty has just asked Stan if he doesn't think that's really gorgeous.

Holy cow, he's touching it again. Clearly, this man knows no fear.

That's the sort of nerve that keeps a player in the game. He's holding it out for Betty to feel. I wonder if she's going to comment on the softness?

She is, Otis, she is! She just compared it to a newborn kitten! Golly Moses, whose side is this woman on?

That's a real blow for Stan. Hang on,

though, because he's about to check the price. Ouch! Did you catch that look? Obviously way too expensive.

But Betty is pointing out the generous yardage—three skeins for an entire sweater! Wham, right in the gut!

Stan says it's still over his yarn budget for the month! Nice block, Stan!

Betty's showing him the "fifteen percent festival discount" sign! This is insane! I don't think he can hold out much longer.

You may be right, Otis. Hey—are you seeing what I'm seeing?

Sweet mother of merino. Folks, you'll never believe this. Hang on to your butts, because the saleswoman has just offered Stan an additional five percent early bird discount.

Possible double-teaming there—are the officials going to allow that? Can we get a call?

No penalty flag, so it looks like they are. And hold the phone—it turns out the colorway is a limited edition.

Whoooooeeeeee. The perfect storm! All he can do is pray for mercy.

It itches

. . . sweet mother of merino . . . folks, you'll never believe this . . . hang on to your butts, because the saleswoman has just offered Stan an additional five percent early bird discount . . .

But Milton, slap my pappy if he isn't turning away—says he has plenty of blue worsted already! He's getting ready to leave the booth! I tell you what, this man must be made of cast iron with a concrete stomach. Ladies and gentlemen, in twenty-five years of yarn shopping I've never seen anything like this.

Betty sure looks mad, doesn't she?

She does indeed. Wait, she's saying something to him now.

Whoa! Betty has told Stan that if he doesn't buy it, she's taking it herself!

A classic Hail Mary! And he's going for it! He's pulled out his credit card! That's it, folks—it's all over for Stan! Tough luck, cowboy, but you sure gave us a thrill. What a fight!

I'm damp from the excitement, Otis. And I kinda wish I'd bought that yarn myself.

You do have quite a weakness for eau de nil, as I recall.

Dang it, you know me too well, buddy.

Stay tuned, folks. Next up we've got Geraldine Tuttle of Wilkinsburg going head-to-head with what may just become her fourteenth spinning wheel.

Yeeeeehaaaaaawwww!

"Ah, yes. That was your Great-aunt Irene.
We no longer speak of Irene. She married an Acrylic."

*"Fire not so big deal. Oog rub two sticks,
make flattering lacy capelet."*

"I want to knit an easy-care sweater for a high-maintenance husband."

"*Frankly, Timmy, my Christmas would be merrier if Mother would learn not to procrastinate.*"

"I can't speak for you, Fred,
but I'm going to be just fine."

"*Some tangling is perfectly normal! Everybody just calm down, unwind, and we'll try the choo-choo train pattern again.*"

Immortality

S CIENCE BOOKS GIVE ALBERT EINSTEIN all the credit for discovering that time is relative, not absolute. He was the first to put it on paper, certainly. But I'd bet my rosewood needles that the basic idea was already familiar to thousands of busy knitters who cast off long before he was born. Being knitters, of course, they didn't have a free hand to write anything down.

For those who don't knit, a minute is absolutely made of sixty brief and equal seconds. Sixty identical minutes make an hour; and twenty-four hours add up to one day. Among knitters, hours and days are just as often measured in rows, pattern repeats, or the number of inches left until the toe of that damned second sock.

A knitter's minute will stretch like cosmic saltwater taffy to fill a year when she's halfway through a lace row of 800 stitches. Then it snaps back to a split second when she considers the number of similar rows remaining before the finished shawl can be blocked, wrapped, and chucked under the Christmas tree.

There are even occasions when time, for us, completely disappears. We think, *just one more row.* Then we glance at the clock a moment later and find we've missed our bedtime, or a dentist appointment, or the month of October.

This year I spent the last two trimesters of my sister's pregnancy working on the baby's christening shawl, a cobwebby Shetland-inspired affair made on needles the size of undernourished toothpicks. For the rest of family, those weeks were an endless agony of anticipation and suspense. I barely noticed them.

What I remember is this. One Saturday in early February, I sat down with a cup of hot Earl Grey to work a bit of the center panel. A few minutes later, I lifted my head to take a sip and the tea was ice cold. And it was April.

I asked my sister whether she would consider crossing her legs and waiting until the shawl was finished. I suggested that an extra month would be sufficient. She suggested I learn to knit faster.

Perhaps because time toys with us so capriciously, we've learned to stick out our tongues at it. While we knit, we're at the mercy of the clock. Once we're finished, though, our work often proves surprisingly durable.

Shakespeare wrote in his Fifty-fifth Sonnet that he expected his words to outlive marble monuments. And sure enough, though great piles of solid rock have crumbled over the centuries his fourteen fragile lines are still with us.

Knitting is similar. We take something apparently delicate and ephemeral—spun fiber—and turn it into objects that may well persist long after our names have been erased from the record.

I did, at last, finish the christening shawl—after the birth, but before the christening. It turned out tolerably well. When shown to the family, it was unanimously declared an heirloom.

An *heirloom*.

That filmy square of silk and cashmere, weighing far less than the beautiful baby we wrapped in it, is expected to outlast me—the too, too solid knitter. And the baby's parents. And even the baby herself. My niece's children may know me, but it's doubtful their children will. They may not even know my name. But they may see this shawl, and know that I lived and loved their grandmother even before she was born, and so translated that love into 180,000 very small stitches.

A knitter's life, measured in the absolute, will last only years and days. But our work, whether it seemed to take an eternity or an eyeblink from cast on to cast off, is the way we stake our claim to immortality.

It itches

51

*"I'm not a cliché, honey. I believe the word
you're looking for is 'classic.'"*

"First, promise me you're not doing this just to get a sweater."

*Studies have shown that experienced
knitters often come to resemble their knitting.*

"I'll be really happy when she gets tired of argyle."

"Mama?"

"In future, Helen, you will kindly stick to the <u>traditional</u> lace patterns."

The Underpants Knitters of Great Fussing-on-the-Wold

———

D EEP IN THE HEART OF THE Yorkshire Dales, unknown to all but the hardiest tourist coaches, lies the tiny—one might almost say itsy-bitsy—village of Great Fussing-on-the-Wold. Today only the name of the pub, Ye Queene's New Knickers, serves to remind that this itsy-bitsy—one might almost say teeny-weeny—village was for generations the most celebrated center of underpants knitting in all of England.

To fully appreciate the famous knitted underpants of Great Fussing, one must begin at the bottom. As there was nothing better to do, the region's inhabitants engaged in sheep farming at least as early as the tenth century. The Domesday Book's entry for the Saxon settlement at Lytle (Little) Fusyng (Fussing) counts 10 villans (villagers) and 200 sheep (sheep).

A marginal note elaborates, "And I hadde rather talke alle daye to ye sheep."

In the mid-sixteenth century, the next era from which records survive, the adjacent villages of Little Fussing and Much Fussing combined to form Great Fussing-on-the-Wold. This sparked a violent riot by the inhabitants, who were extremely reluctant to have all their stationery reprinted. An angry mob smashed the mill, slaughtered cattle and set fire to most of the barns before recovering its senses and feeling very silly indeed.

Great Fussing might not have survived the loss of livelihood but for the quick thinking of the local squire, Willoughby Fitzbadleigh. Squire Willoughby ordered the village spinsters to turn the finest of the spring wool clip—traditionally reserved for dessert topping—into a thread of surpassing luster and softness. This was given to Great Fussing's champion knitter, known to history only as Miss Thelma Lou "Midge" Bracegirdle of 14 Marigold Terrace. She fashioned from it a pair of luxurious underpants which the squire contrived to have presented at court to Queen Elizabeth I.

Elizabeth's reaction was recorded by a lady of the household in her daily account of the royal unmentionables.

> Her Majestee receev'd ye nether pantys with greet delyte and retir'd at once to here chambere for to treye them oon. So happilee did they laye upon the royall bum-bumme that shee did saye nevere wood she weare any ladye pantys of othere make and shee did command seven payre of ye same in divers colors with ye dayes of ye weeke embroydr'd thereuponne.

Thus with a single mail order Elizabeth saved Great Fussing from poverty, and ushered in what history now regards as the Golden Age of Knitted Underpants. Squire Willoughby was created a knight, and he adopted a coat of arms

. . . thus with a single mail order Elizabeth ushered in what history now regards as the Golden Age of Knitted Underpants.

with the motto *E Clunibus Reginae Surgo*, or *I Rise from the Queen's Bottom*.

The villagers were inundated by frantic requests from court gentry for their own copies of the queen's preferred underwear. Entire families went to work meeting the demand. Children as young as four years were taught to knit simple waistbands using a charming country rhyme about "Lusty Sally" and her "peekaboo britches," which out of respect for the delicacy of the modern reader we forbear to quote in full.

The form of the underpants, or "wooly mittens" as the villagers called them in order to confuse historians, remained unchanged for nearly two hundred years. Each pair was worked from the top down on a set of eight double-pointed needles, fashioned by the knitter from alder, ash, or plastic picnic forks according to personal preference. Lace edgings were particular to each family and recipes were closely guarded; edging thieves, if caught, were exposed in the village stocks with balls of yarn stuck up their noses.

Within a decade, the public's appetite for the famous "fussy pantys" of Yorkshire grew overwhelming; production spread from Great Fussing to the neighboring villages of Constant Whining and Fret. So central did knitting become to the region's economy that knitters transformed a pagan fertility ceremony into the "running of the gusset" before the annual fair. To ensure a bountiful season, children chased a ewe lamb dressed in red britches around and around the market square, chanting

> *I see London*
> *I see France*
> *We make fancy*
> *Underpants*

until the lamb, annoyed and exhausted, collapsed and was made into souvlaki. The picturesque rite persists to this day, though due to stricter animal welfare laws the children now run behind a large piece of tofu pulled on a string.

Aside from a brief eclipse during the notoriously itchy Puritan Protectorate (which declared soft underclothes an incentive to sin) the knitters of Great Fussing enjoyed royal patronage and popular acclaim until the nineteenth century, when the arrival of cheap, machine-made underpants dealt the industry its deathblow. A scattering of cottagers continued to produce items for the tourist trade, though these were often of inferior quality and frequently left crotchless to save yarn and labor.

The last of the professional underpants knitters died in 1914 and was buried without ceremony in the churchyard at Great Fussing. Her touching epitaph serves as a fitting tribute to all whose busy needles once brought renown to a forgotten corner of England:

> *Erected in memory*
> *Of the knitter Olive Croft.*
> *Her fingers were nimble*
> *And her knickers were soft.*

"Leonard, you'll <u>never</u> guess what I did at the fiber festival."

"Because it relaxes me, that's why!"

"*I don't know which to buy. We're at that awkward stage where I love him more than alpaca, but less than cashmere.*"

"That's the same cable I used in Dylan's baby blanket."

It itches

"Charlie, please try to understand. You're English.
I'm Continental. And I just don't believe in mixed marriages."

"It's 100% eco-friendly hypoallergenic organic recycled fiber, spun and hand-dyed by a fair-trade worker-owned collective in a developing nation. Unfortunately, it also itches like hell."

Advice from a Poncho

H ELLO, AGAIN. NICE TO SEE YOU. It's been dull, terribly dull, sitting for thirty years in a cardboard box on the very top shelf in the darkest corner of the basement.

You must be surprised to find me. I'm not what you're looking for, am I? Probably you're looking for your old scrapbook. Here it is. I can't tell you how often I've read all the way through it. There's been plenty of time, sitting in a cardboard box on the very top shelf in the darkest corner of the basement for thirty years. But who's counting?

Would you mind if we went upstairs for a little sunlight and fresh air? It would do me good. It would also do me good if you'd see to the mildew problem down here, but don't worry— I know you're busy. I don't judge.

Don't know what to say, do you? I'm sure you didn't remember me being so colorful. Well, it's not *my* fault. Who chose these colors? You did. Who wished for me in the first place? You did.

Look at page six of the scrapbook. There's a photograph of you with your two best friends in the fall of 1975. They're wearing ponchos. You're not. You were the odd girl out: the only eight-year-old in your entire school—possibly in the entire *world*—without her own poncho.

Your mother didn't think this was a tragedy, but your grandmother understood. She'd grown up during the Great Depression wearing nothing but hand-me-downs. Painful. She decided that you would have your poncho, made to order.

By 1975 she'd already been knitting for fifty years. All the girls in her family had to learn some kind of needlework. Times were tough. If you couldn't make it, you couldn't have it. More often than not you were making it for somebody else, who might or might not appreciate what you had done.

Your grandmother was lucky. Praise or none, she enjoyed sitting quietly with her needles, and especially in winter the demands of sock knitting and sock mending often excused her from kitchen work. She hated kitchen work.

But she loved to knit. All through the war she turned out socks for soldiers, and occasionally something pretty for herself. It made her feel useful, and helped to calm her nerves while she worried over two brothers and one dear friend—your future grandfather—who were overseas and might never come home.

After the war, everything changed. Your grandmother's sisters stuffed their workbaskets into the closet and swore they'd never look at another mended or home-sewn dress. The Depression was over. America was rich. Why work your fingers to the bone when you could go to the store and buy whatever you wanted?

Your grandmother left home to marry your grandfather, and she fell in love with the push-button conveniences in the new house. But she kept knitting, even though she began to feel self-conscious about it.

Before the war it was no problem to bring out her needles after sup-

. . . color was not your strong suit. You selected deep purple, pumpkin orange, and this disgusting shade of bile green.

per when everyone gathered in the kitchen. Now everybody sat in the living room around the television and they made remarks. "Put that down," they'd say. "You're missing the program!"

It made no sense. As a girl, she'd been expected to re-heel socks while also watching the soup and her baby brother. Did *Your Hit Parade* really require her full attention?

By the late 1960s she wouldn't knit if anybody but immediate family was in the room. Nobody cared what she was

making anyhow. None of it was necessary. Socks were cheap as paper, and at age twelve your mother made it clear that sending her to school in a handknit sweater was a form of child abuse.

For a little while she gave it up, but her empty hands shook. Her brain felt empty, too, with nothing to fill it except soap operas and women's magazines. Since there was nothing useful to knit, she turned to the useless: luncheon sets too fancy to put on the table, covers for the spare roll of toilet paper, an endless parade of Christmas tree ornaments. Anything to keep her fingers and her mind engaged.

Yarn had changed, too. You couldn't get good, solid wools at the variety store any more, but if the projects didn't matter, why be particular about the yarn?

Your mother refused to learn to knit. She wished your grandmother would stop. It was pathetic, said your mother, for a smart woman to fritter her life away in a chair. And it was difficult to know what to do with all the luncheon sets and toilet paper covers.

When you asked for a poncho, you were the first person since the 1940s to specially request a piece of knitting. And so you found yourself in the yarn aisle at the craft store so fast that you weren't quite sure how you got there. "Go ahead," said Grandma. "Pick the three colors you like best and that's what I'll use. Any three."

Apparently color was not your strong suit. You selected deep purple, pumpkin orange, and this disgusting shade of bile green. The combination gave her a migraine, but she never complained. She was just happy her work was wanted again.

You stood by as she made a good portion of me. You even learned to knit a sloppy stitch or two. Then you got bored and ran outside and forgot—but not completely. Something stirred inside years later when you read an article about how knitting— poor old dowdy, despised knitting— had become the hobby of choice for the world's most sophisticated, opinionated, progressive women. Then you remembered watching me grow and the joy of putting something on your shoulders that had been made just for you, just as you liked.

You came down to the basement and dug around until you found her needles, which even your mother couldn't bear to throw away. You got some yarn, and a book, and a group;

. . . sort of makes you want to frame me and hang me on the wall, doesn't it?

and you became what your grand-mother never dreamed you would be: a knitter.

Now your stash is packed with better wool and finer needles than any she ever saw. Your pullovers are prized possessions, and your baby blankets are the talk of the shower. It will take years to knit all the socks you've been asked for.

I, on the other hand, am hidden in the darkest corner of the basement.

Does that seem fair? After all, every-thing your grandmother knew passed through me to reach you. I'm not just a bile green poncho; I'm part of your history. A sacred relic. A conduit of knowledge.

Sort of makes you want to frame me and hang me on the wall, doesn't it?

Oh, well. I tried. Before you close the box again, though, would you mind throwing in a couple of new magazines? Thirty years is a long time.

"Hand over the poncho."

FRANKLIN

"And then she bound off loosely on a wrong side row, keeping all stitches in pattern, and they lived happily ever after."

"Yeah, it's unusual. But a mutual love of good yarn conquers all."

Free-Range Knitters

"Now that the kids are out of the house, maybe I could fill the gap with a couple of Blue-Faced Leicesters."

"Bummer."

"Attention, please. I need the two skeins of red alpaca to
be returned to the knitting basket as soon as possible.
No questions will be asked."

"*Next, say hello to lifelong knitter Annie Livingstone of Billings, Montana. Annie has three children, seven grandchildren and two great-grandchildren, and has never knit a darn thing for any one of them.*"

*"It works fine, except when I start a new Fair Isle project.
Then my husband can't keep his hands off me."*

The Knit Stitch: Theme & Variations

—

I N AN ERA OF NICHE MARKETING, even the classics must change or perish.

Theme
In through the front door,
Run around the back.
Peek through the window,
And off jumps Jack.

Variation the First:
For the Tired Executive
Out through the front door
Into the car,
Peek at the office,
Leave for the bar.

Variation the Second:
For the Eco-Tourist
Go to Madagascar
Run around the lemur.
Leave Madagascar
Before you break a femur.

Variation the Third:
For Those in Need of Exercise
Up from the easy chair,
Run around the yard,
Back to the easy chair,
Breathing very hard.

Variation the Fourth:
For the Busy Diplomat
Enter through security,
Sprint to the gate,
Jump in the airplane,
Fly to the United Arab Emirates.

Variation the Fifth:
For the Mobster
Go to the warehouse,
Pick up the stiff.
Dip him in the concrete,
Drop him off the cliff.

Variation the Sixth:
For Unlucky Rabbits.
Or Lucky Hunters.
Out of the burrow,
Hop around the yew,
Meet up with a hunter,
Wind up in a stew.

Variation the Seventh:
For the Mother Who Has Everything,
With Love
Go to the fiber farm,
Pick up a llama.
Bring it back home
And give it to Mama.

"Okay, Joe, now pay attention. In through the front door. Right.
Run around the back. No, the back. The <u>back</u>. Yep. Okay, now
peep through the window—yeah, like that—and off jumps Jack."

"Our Loyal Customer program entitles you to a discount and a free tote bag after purchases equal to fifteen percent of your adjusted gross income."

*"The minute his back is turned, I call
dibs on the lime green worsted."*

"I don't know art, but I know I wouldn't want to knit a sweater for it."

"Aye, miss. Most o' the sheep in these parts belongs to Mister Fassett."

"We agreed that I'd cut back on yarn if he'd cut back on beer, so I figure I'm safe at least until the end of football season."

Knittin' with a Whip

———

I KNOW A WOMAN WHO LIKES TO talk at length about how knitting is a form of meditation. Usually it happens after a second glass of red wine. Her eyelids droop and she starts speaking in italics. *"The gentle click of the needles. The reassuring repetition of the stitches. They transport your inner being to a place of peace. A place beyond worry."*

It would be rude to tip the canoe while she's paddling to nirvana, so I've never told her my dirty secret: I don't always knit to relax. I like knitting best when it hurts.

I see my needles the way a dedicated masochist sees his collection of whips and manacles—as treasured instruments of delicious torture. Grandma would probably blame it on the general cussedness she noticed when I was just a boy. "You always want to do everything the hard way," she said, and she was right. Don't throw me in the briar patch. Just lead me to the scenic overlook and I'll jump.

I started knitting the same way most folks do: fat yarn, big needles, garter stitch. Easy. Knit, knit, knit, knit, knit. Turn. Knit, knit, knit, knit, knit. Yawn.

My soul was not on fire. I didn't want knitting to be easy; I wanted it to be flashy and complex, like a clockwork Fabergé egg. I'm a guy. I like to show off. I'm less interested in cute mittens than in bragging rights.

So I wandered from the neatly swept path of stockinette into beds of spicy, exotic delights like jacquard, entrelac, and Aran cables. At the center of the poisoned garden grew the ultimate *fleur du mal*, lace knitting—many-branched, thorn laden, and irresistible. I fell to my knees at first sight of a Shetland shawl, six feet square and worked on impossibly skinny needles. "Please," I whimpered. "Please, let me knit you."

Lace, it turned out, was a cruel mistress who insisted on absolute submission. Within a few months I was a cross-eyed and battered wreck, finally driven to the brink by a sadistic Estonian doily that demanded I purl five together until my fingers bled. Feeling defiant, I threw the whole snarled mess across the room. And then I apologized. I apologized, out loud, to my knitting.

I had hit bottom. Or so I thought.

I decided to take it easy for a bit, maybe even try a little innocent crochet. Searching the library for a kinder companion, I turned up a book from the 1960s that claimed to be full of Victorian knitting patterns.

It wasn't. It was full of the author's clunky, simplified interpretations of Victorian knitting patterns. There were mouthwatering photographs of original, nineteenth-century pieces, but these, she insisted, were beyond my reach. "The busy modern knitter," she wrote, "has neither the time nor the patience to devote herself to such complicated work."

She might as well have slapped my

. . . choosing **suitable** yarn requires **guesswork** . . . chances are your local shop doesn't **stock** the "No. 30 **Mee's** Persian thread."

face with her glove.

I began a fevered search for original pattern sources. Beautiful they turned out to be—juicy, aromatic volumes with deceptively sweet titles like *The Knitter's Friend*, often demurely attributed to "A Lady."

However, these guides to the gentle art of needlework aren't exactly gentle. They're products of the Victorian era, which also brought us Gatling guns, colonial genocide, and child factory labor. The Victorians knew a thing or two about cruelty, and where modern pattern writers take you tenderly by the hand, the "ladies" will more often push you down the stairs.

Of course, I was instantly smitten.

Using a nineteenth-century knitting book is like doing the Highland fling in a minefield. No matter how carefully you step, you're going to wind up shattered at least once before the jig is finished.

For example, selecting a project is tricky when you can't figure out what the hell half the patterns are for. Should I make a *fascinator* or a *tidy?* A *zephyr?* Maybe a *muffatee?* How about a *bosom friend?* Even if I finished making the bosom friend I'm not sure I'd know how to wear it, though I think I have an idea of where it's supposed to go.

Choosing suitable yarn requires guesswork. Chances are your local shop doesn't stock the "No. 30 Mee's Persian thread" called for in Cornelia Mee's 1844 recipe for a lace edging. Needle sizes are usually specified with number systems as obsolete as the Code of Hammurabi, or left wide open to interpretation. Which do you think is larger, "good sized" or "not too thick"?

And before you cast on, I recommend a crash course in ye olde knitting lingo:

A "needle" may have two pointy ends or one. A "pin" usually has only one point, but may have two. Often the meaning is unclear, and you have the fun of guessing.

A purl may be a purl, or it may be a "pearl," a "turn," a "welt" or a "seam"—even within the same pattern. "Seam" may also mean a sewn seam or a series of purl stitches. Often, you have the fun of guessing.

"Take a stitch" means to knit a stitch, or it may mean to pick up a stitch, or it may mean to knit two stitches together. Often, you have the fun of guessing.

To indicate a yarn over, the writer may specify that you bring it forward, between, up and over, or around. She may or may not expect you to work a corresponding decrease afterwards. Often, you have the fun of . . . are you sensing a trend?

And then there are the instructions, sometimes written with an opaque minimalism guaranteed to reduce even strong knitters to tears. Here's a muffatee pattern, unabridged, from the 1840 edition of the anonymous compendium, *The Workwoman's Guide*.

> *This is in plain knitting.*
> *Set on twenty stitches,*
> *Knit twenty eight ribs.*
> *Fringe is sewed on with a carpet*
> *needle in a kind of cross stitch,*
> *being wound over a mesh of the*
> *proper width.*

That's all the help you get, sister.

But nobody turns the thumbscrews quite like Cornelia Mee, who from the 1840s through the 1860s cranked out a pile of bestsellers on knitting and crochet. Her recipe "For a Turkish Cushion," printed in the 1844 *Mee's Companion to the Work-Table*, is a masterpiece of literary sadism in three sentences.

She begins quietly with instructions to cast on 90 stitches and work a simple slip-stitched texture pattern across the row. In the second sentence, with the knitter already ensnared, she takes off the mask to reveal the demon succubus:

> *The whole of the knitting is done*
> *in this manner; then knit 2 rows*
> *of the dark for the edge, 2 rows of*
> *the colour for the centre, 2 more*
> *dark: these six rows form an edge,*
> *which is done on each side of each*
> *piece. Then commence the centre,*
> *and knit 2 rows to the end, in*
> *the 3d row, leave 6 stitches at the*
> *end, and turn back, as if begin-*
> *ning a fresh row . . .*

Got that? She continues for seven lines barely pausing for breath, dragging her victim deep into the labyrinth before slamming the dungeon door on his fingers with the final sentence:

> *This completes 1 piece,*
> *16 of which are required.*

Oh, Mistress Cornelia, how I worship you. It hurts so good.

"I can't talk right now, Chris. I'm having a violent
disagreement with a skein of mohair."

It itches

95

"Leroy! Stop the car!"

"Isn't it a hoot, Carol? I'm turning into
a little old peasant woman."

"I know perfectly well what He told you, dearest. And now <u>I'm</u> telling you that I won't get into that thing without my stash."

"I don't understand how you can just sit there knitting all day."

It itches

"My goodness, Grandma! What a big stereotype you are!"

"Oh, please. Ever since she discovered that damned Barbara Walker there's no talking to her."

It's a Guy Thing

WHEN YOU'RE A GUY WHO knits and you do your thing in public, you become ambassador-at-large for all guys who knit. There's a popular assumption that we think and act as one, like the Communist Party or the Dallas Cowboys Cheerleaders. I, however, feel unable to speak for the entire tribe when I'm asked what it feels like for a boy, so I decided to collect opinions at Men's Knitting Night.

Our group meets twice a month in the back room at the Twisted Stitch, a grungy knitter bar on 28th Street in the Fleece District. We're a motley crowd —all you need to do is look at us to know that all men who knit are not alike. And I hate to name-drop, but there are a few celebrity regulars. On this particular night, eight of us turned up: myself, George, Schuyler, Santa Claus, and the Four Horsemen of the Apocalypse—War, Famine, Pestilence, and Death.

"I hope you're hungry," said Famine, setting a foil-covered tray on the center of the table.

"Please tell me those are your homemade brownies," said Santa.

"Sorry—butterscotch squares," said Famine.

"Good enough," said Santa.

We each grabbed a cookie and I got down to business.

"What do you guys say," I asked, "when somebody asks you why you knit?"

Santa laughed. "I tell them my alternatives are talking shop with a bunch of elves or listening to my wife complain about the weather."

"Maybe she needs to learn to knit," said George.

"I wish she would," said Santa. "I tried to teach her and she quit after half a scarf. She says doesn't have the patience to sit still for so long. But she'll spend six hours at the computer eating cookies and looking for retirement properties in Florida. I don't get it."

We each nodded in sympathy. We'd been there.

"Knitting calms me down," said War. "I feel fidgety if my hands aren't busy, and I get into trouble."

"No kidding," said Pestilence. "Once, he forgot to pack yarn for a flight to Bermuda and by the time we landed the Russians had invaded Afghanistan."

Schuyler put down his earflap hat and took a thoughtful sip of chai latte. "I guess I do it because I like subverting mass production and the culture of consumption. No offense, dude."

"None taken," said Santa.

"These sound like the same reasons a lot of women knit," I said. "Do you think there are any special thrills we get from it that they don't?"

"I admit," said Pestilence, "I like the attention that comes with knitting in public. I'm such a novelty, I don't even have to be working on anything cool. Three inches of garter stitch and the chicks are on me like a swarm of killer bees."

George disagreed. "I hate it when strangers do that. They always tap my shoulder when I'm counting and tell me they're so impressed, even if I'm making a stupid dishcloth, because I'm a man— and yet *somehow* I can knit! They think it's so *cute*."

"Dang it," muttered Death, "I twisted a cable the wrong way six rounds ago."

"Harsh," said Schuyler.

"It's okay," said Death. "I actually enjoy ripping back."

"Do you think we approach knitting differently than women do?" I asked.

"We worry less about the boyfriend sweater curse," said Famine.

"Says you," said Schuyler.

"Fine," said Death. "We don't have to know about bust darts."

"Says you, Mister Skinny," growled Santa.

"Excuse me for living," said Death. He turned to me. "What do you think? Is it any different for you than it is for the female knitters you know?"

Suddenly, epiphany.

"Perhaps," I said, "the joys of knitting transcend gender. The joy of creating. The joy of learning. The joy of sharing. The joy of friendship."

"Dude," said War, "are you drunk?"

Something fluttered across the table and landed on George's ball of sock yarn. Everybody froze.

Schuyler gasped. "Is that—"

"A moth," said Death grimly. "Some-body's infested. Again."

We all looked at Pestilence, who was hastily stuffing half a mitten back into his bag. "Occupational hazard," he said sheepishly.

The meeting adjourned in awkward silence. Pestilence galloped away without saying goodbye.

The next day I saw my friend Midge at the yarn store and told her what had happened. She was appalled.

"I can't believe you let a buddy go cope with a recurring moth problem all by himself," she said.

"He needed space!" I said.

"You couldn't be a little supportive? Ask if he wanted to talk? Give him a hug and tell him you found eggs in your best sweater on New Year's Eve?"

"Well . . . we all chipped in and bought him a T-shirt that says 'Bug Boy.' Does that count?"

"What the heck is wrong with you?"

"It's a guy thing," I told her. "You wouldn't understand."

*Kathy and Selma realized this was
a pivotal moment in their friendship.*

"Wow! Cashmere!"

"Gimme a break, guys. Like straw and twigs are <u>so</u> practical."

"Two hundred hours, one hundred thousand stitches,
and I still end up humiliated in front of the entire
county by a pink angora shrug."

FRANKLIN

It itches

"Each ball is hand-rolled around a
choice morsel of dead bird."

get your knitting fix

with these resources from Interweave

Are you knitting daily?

knittingdaily
where life meets knitting

Join **KnittingDaily.com,** an online community that shares your passion for knitting. You'll get a free e-newsletter, free patterns, a daily blog, event updates, project store, galleries, tips and techniques, and more. Sign up for *Knitting Daily* at **knittingdaily.com.**

From cover to cover, *Interweave Knits* magazine presents great projects for the beginner to the advanced knitter. Every issue is packed full of captivating smart designs, step-by-step instructions, easy-to-understand illustrations, plus well-written, lively articles sure to inspire.

interweaveknits.com

INTERWEAVE
KNITS